Discover
the **Diamond** in
You

Discover the Diamond in You

THE *59* MINUTE GUIDE TO SUCCESS!

Foreword by the Success Icon of a Billion Hearts!
SHAH RUKH KHAN!!!

Arindam Chaudhuri

Vikas®Publishing House Pvt Ltd

VIKAS® PUBLISHING HOUSE PVT LTD

E-28, Sector-8, **Noida**-201301 (UP)
Phone: 0120-4078900 • Fax: 4078999
VIKAS® Regd. Office: 576, Masjid Road, Jangpura, **New Delhi**-110 014

E-mail: helpline@vikaspublishing.com • *www.vikaspublishing.com*

- First Floor, N.S. Bhawan, 4th Cross, 4th Main, Gandhi Nagar,
  Bengaluru-560 009 • Phone: 080-22204639, 22281254
- Damodhar Centre, New No. 62, Old No. 59, Nelson Manickam Road,
  Aminjikarai, **Chennai**-600 029 • Phone: 044-23744547, 23746090
- P-51/1, CIT Road, Scheme - 52, **Kolkata**-700014
  • Ph. 033-22866995, 22866996
- 67/68, 3rd Floor, Aditya Industrial Estate, Chincholi Bunder, Malad (West),
  Mumbai-400 064 • Ph. 022-28772545, 28768301

Distributors:

UBS PUBLISHERS' DISTRIBUTORS PVT LTD

5, Ansari Road, **New Delhi**-110 002
  • Ph. 011-23273601, 23266646 • Fax: 23276593, 23274261
- 10, First Main Road, Gandhi Nagar, **Bengaluru**-560 009 • Ph. 080-22253903
- Z-18, M P Nagar, Zone-1, **Bhopal**-462 011 • Ph. 0755-4203183, 4203193
- Ist Floor 145, Cuttack Road, **Bhubaneshwar**-751 006 • Ph. 0674-2314446
- 60, Nelson Manickam Road, Aminjikarai, **Chennai**-600 029 • Ph. 044-23746222
- 2nd & 3rd Floor, Sri Guru Towers, No. 1-7, Sathy Road,
  Cross III, Gandhipuram, **Coimbatore**-641 012
- 40/7940, Convent Road, **Ernakulam**-682 035 • Ph. 0484-2353901, 2363905
- 3rd Floor, Alekhya Jagadish Chambers, H. No. 4-1-1058, Boggulkunta, Tilak Road,
  Hyderabad-500 001 • Ph. 040-24754472 / 73 / 74
- 8/1-B, Chowringhee Lane, **Kolkata**-700 016 • Ph. 033-22521821, 22522910
- 9 Ashok Nagar, Near Pratibha Press, Gautam Buddha Marg, Latush Road,
  Lucknow-226 001 • Ph. 0522-2294134, 3014010
- 2nd Floor, Apeejay Chambers, 5 Wallace Street, Fort, **Mumbai**-400 001
  • Ph. 022-66376922-3, 66102069 • Fax: 66376921
- GF, Western Side, Annapoorna Complex, Naya Tola, **Patna**-800 004
  • Ph. 0612-2672856, 2673973
- 680 Budhwar Peth, 2nd Floor, Appa Balwant Chowk, **Pune**-411 002
  • Ph. 020-24461653, 24433976

VIKAS® is the registered trademark of Vikas® Publishing House Pvt Ltd
Copyright © Arindam Chaudhuri, 2009

Printed at Millennium Offset Pvt Ltd, New Delhi-110028

Praise for Arindam Chaudhuri

"The maverick management guru!"
Financial Times, London

"The intellectual litterateur of the decade"
The Hindustan Times

"Set(s) the stage on fire"
"Inspiration personified"
The Times of India

Also by Arindam Chaudhuri

PLANNING INDIA

COUNT YOUR CHICKENS
BEFORE THEY HATCH

THE GREAT INDIAN DREAM

Praise for
'Discover the Diamond in You'

"No quick fixes, this book is packed with sound, simple and realistic advice. It reveals and guides one with clarity and in-depth searching, making one conscious of one's own potential, thereby empowering and motivating each individual to experience true fulfillment."

AMITABH BACHCHAN
Voted as the millennium's "Greatest Actor of Stage and Screen" in a poll by BBC News

FOR MY FATHER

This one is for you, Baba! You have always taught me economics and shown me the way to understand the world better. But you have no clue that you have always inspired me as much with your entrepreneurial vision. And it's from you that I learnt, "If you think you can, you are right." This book is to that spirit in you that believes that we are all diamonds – at the most, just waiting to be discovered! This book is also to the spirit of the great IIPM education movement that you started, which has created so many sparkling diamonds!

PREFACE

Why this book: My earlier book, *Count Your Chickens Before They Hatch*, was a book on success indeed, but perhaps more from a managerial perspective. My friends have been telling me since then to write a book on success, but without any management theories! This book, thus, is an attempt to fulfill the desires of my friends and therefore, is, also in a way *Count Your Chickens Before They Hatch, Part II.*

This book is also an attempt to share the last eight years of my learnings since *Count Your Chickens Before They Hatch*! It attempts to share with my readers powerful principles of success that I've grown to passionately believe in; to share some secrets I've seen around me, that have led to success in life. And above all, it's an attempt to induce the belief in my readers that they are all gems – precious gems. In fact diamonds, which at times are just waiting to be discovered.

For whom is this book: This book is for everybody. Everybody who wants to increase his or her productivity in life and work. Everybody who wants to be a better father, mother, sister, brother, son, daughter, manager or entrepreneur! For we are all diamonds waiting to be discovered or cut, or polished or to dazzle. And at times perhaps, diamonds which have lost a bit of sheen; it's only by regular polishing that we remain the diamonds that we always were.

Whom do I owe this book to: I owe almost everything that I am to my father. His pure and passionate commitment to working and thinking non-stop about how to remove poverty from India and the world is inspirational beyond what words can explain. When you grow up seeing a man who has never ever spoken or thought of anything else but his country and its poor, and has spent an entire life working only for them, then obviously all you can feel is absolute awe. I actually owe an apology to him for doing many things, which he wouldn't have wanted me to do – like making his part of the house a little bit more modern (my parents and my family stay together), unlike the Ho Chi Minh type of living and setting that he had always aspired for. However, I owe him a promise that I will try my level best to fulfil all his dreams of seeing an India without the problems it has in the areas of health, education, employment and justice. And as a minute token of this promise of mine, the entire proceeds of this book will go completely to his 'Manav Seva Kendra' centres that he runs with unseen and unbelievable passion in the villages within West Bengal and Orissa.

Acknowledgements to my most important partner: Often, I fail to acknowledge this or I assume that it is understood. But this time, I won't make that mistake. Because I genuinely feel that without the support of my wife and friend Rajita, I wouldn't have been doing half the things I do with half the peace. And more than that, without having a friend who always and without fail provides intellectual companionship with so much honesty and dedication, I would really have been incomplete! Rajita, you really never ask for any diamonds, but are the real diamond of my life :-) Thanks for all your support in life and for the extensive support in the making of this book!

Thank you Shah Rukh! My father still remembers you as Abhimanyu Rai from *Fauji*! I remember going with Rajita, time after time to watch *Dilwale Dulhaniya Le Jayenge*, only to come back with an increased appetite for you. You are indeed the icon of a billion hearts as well as the few in our home! But what is most fascinating about you is that you are the rarest combination of success and intelligence. It's just amazing to hear you speak – almost on any topic. The day I heard you speak on success at IIPM for the first time, I had this strong urge to have the foreword of my book penned by you! It's really an honour for me that you agreed to share your most inspiring thoughts in spite of the fact that these very thoughts will also find a reflection in your forthcoming autobiography!!!

I also owe my happiness to: My family: my mom Ratna – a gem; my sister Arundhati – a star; and my son Che – my diamond! Thanks for the love you all give to keep me going. I must also thank my friends Ashok, Sandeep, Prashanto, Shikha, Aditi and their respective family members Uma, Anjali, Monalisa, Esha and my '*jaan*' Sarah for providing me unparalleled happiness all the time. My heartfelt thanks to my colleagues too, who keep my life and work full of happiness, especially during tough times. They are all absolute diamonds. My friend and colleague A. Sandeep who is always there for me (and also edited this book), come what may; my organisation's backbone – Amit and Prasun, my most trusted warriors; Naveen, who coaxed me to keep this the title of the book; the ever-inspiring Sourav; my creative brain Shubho; my most driven colleagues Deepak, Rakesh, Shouvik, Rahul, Vikram, Viraj (who, being the son of a gemologist, explained to me the intricacies of diamonds), Rajat. S, Anirudh and Sumit; my intellectual support Sutanu; my one-man advisory team Sudhir; my senior colleagues Namita, Satyajit, Arindam, Rajat and Abhimanyu; and my colleagues Biswajit and Shantanu for their creative help in designing this book. Piyush, thanks for being such a sweet friend and always giving me the support of your lovely publishing house, Vikas Publishing! I thank all my other colleagues, friends and well-wishers whose love always makes me feel like a diamond!

Lastly, not a day goes by when I don't miss you Aurobindo, my brother. You were the rarest diamond of our lives.

Why is this book also referred to as the 59 minute guide to success: That is because after the foreword, there are only 59 written pages in this book and it shouldn't take any reader more than one minute to read, understand and grasp each page. Once you have read and understood these pages, the process of discovering the diamond in you will be complete! How much you dazzle thereafter in life would depend upon how much you practise the powerful principles discussed in this book!

Now go ahead and, "Discover The Diamond In You!"

Trivia: I run my entire firm virtually on sms as I don't use e-mail. I find typing an sms the fastest way of communicating. Every week, I write my editorials for my magazine The Sunday Indian *on sms. It might sound unbelievable but yes, it's true that I typed the entire book on my mobile and kept forwarding the messages to my colleague Biswajit, who then put it into the book format.*

Contents

Success is never final just like failure is never fatal

FOREWORD

Arindam is a dear friend and I have enjoyed reading his books and articles. This one, which you are holding in your hands, I can assure you is a real diamond – and therefore, for me, it is a privilege to write this foreword! The book talks lucidly about the meaning of success and principles that will help you become successful. I realize that I am expected to write about success as the world usually sees me as a successful person. But instead, I would rather write about the other end of the spectrum . . . that is, failure! Unless you know what you want to avoid, I think it is very difficult to get what you wish to obtain.

I believe that success is a wonderful experience, but not always one from which we acquire wisdom or knowledge – which is why I feel success, whether deserving or not, can be enjoyed but cannot be passed on. My being successful in no way guarantees that my children will be successful too! So instead of trying to write about success and how to become successful, let me tell you honestly all that I have gone through in life.

I'm very scared of failures. In my life, it's not success that I want as much as I want to not fail. I have seen a lot of failures. Mine was a normal, lower-middle class family. My father was a beautiful man and the most successful failure in the world. My mother also failed to stay with me long enough for her to see me become a movie star. Actually, we were very poor, and at a very early age — after my parents died — I equated poverty with failure. Whether it was right or wrong, I knew just one fact — I never wanted to be poor. When I signed my initial films, most of them were discards of actors; films, for which producers could not find anyone to act. I acted in all of them just to make sure that I continued working and avoided unemployment. I worked very hard on those movies out of desperation and belief — sentiments that somehow go hand in hand. Somehow, something worked, and suddenly I was a big star! I guess the fear of failure, in the context of what I knew it to be, always made me give more than a hundred per cent wherever and whenever I could. Failure gave me an incentive to work harder, an act which invariably leads to some kind of success in most cases.

So work hard whenever you fail. Failure is an amazing teacher. If you don't fail, you will never learn. If you don't learn, you will never grow and never really discover the diamond inside you! Failure taught me to stop pretending and being someone else. It gave me a clear sense of direction. Sometimes, you are not cut out for a particular job and you have to accept it and leave it. You need to know when to stop beating a dead horse, and repeated failure at something can sometimes be the best sign and time to do so. Failure helped me find real friends and test out the true strengths of relationships. It taught me empathy towards others. Being a star, it is easy for me to be prone to the notion that I am superior, good looking, fantastic, the 'King of Bollywood' – but some films just happened. And I realized with honesty that what I become is simply based on what I do. I am neither special nor immune to the results of bad work or bad ideas . . . I'm just like everyone else. Failure also helped me to discover that I had a stronger will and more discipline than I had suspected, and these helped me wake up each morning with a passion to strive harder.

I won't say failure is a good thing, but I would like to tell you all that life is not just a checklist of acquisitions, achievements and fulfillments. Your qualifications and CV don't matter. Instead, life is difficult and complicated and beyond anyone's control. The humility to know that and the ability to respect your failures will help you survive life's unknown qualities and quantities. The 9Ps of success that Arindam so swiftly and lucidly narrates will help you overcome failures and achieve success — because we all need some guidelines when we are down.

Remember, success is never final, just like failure is never fatal! Courage is doing what you are afraid to do. There can be no courage, unless you are scared. Have the fear of failure, so that you all get the courage to succeed! This book is guaranteed to inspire you and it will definitely get you started on your path to discover the diamond within. There is a lifetime of learning squeezed into this innovative book. 59 minutes is all Arindam asks from you and you will have a more positive approach to your life forever. I finished this book in 59 minutes flat and it read like a story I have often lived and experienced. You too will discover a part of yourself in these pages and get inspired. Read on to have some control over the future course of your life — because this control will bring success within your sights.

All the best!

Shah Rukh Khan

You know what you are, but you don't know what you can become!

Yes! You are a diamond! Just the way diamonds are rare, so are humans. While diamonds are found only in rare places on earth, similar is the case with life, which is found only in the rarest of rare places in our solar system – in fact, earth is the only such place known to me. And amongst the thousands of different types of life, being born as a human being is no less than being a diamond in a coal mine! The question therefore is not whether you are a diamond, but which stage you are in? It could even be that you are yet to discover it – in fact, most of us live life without discovering that we have a diamond within us! At times, even when we realise that there is a diamond in us, we never bother to cut it properly; or rather, fail to get the right teachers who can cut the various edges properly and bring out the light inside. At times, we discover the diamond, and even cut it, but fail to polish it properly; for it's only when we polish a well-cut diamond properly that it starts to dazzle! And some of us are diamonds that may have just lost their sheen a little and require some more polishing. But it's my firm belief that we are all diamonds in this world! It's with this belief that we run our institute IIPM. The first day, every student is told that he is a diamond and he must believe that he is. And that in the institute, we will cut and polish him from 72 different edges – there are 72 subjects that are taught in a typical programme at IIPM – till he is finally ready to dazzle! And do they dazzle before leaving!!!

This book is about the entire process of the discovery to dazzle! It helps you explore and discover the diamond within you – which is most important! It also tells you how to cut and polish the diamond, so that you finally dazzle like a rare gem. To believe that you are a diamond, you have to believe that you are rare. You have to believe that you can dazzle, once shown the right path. And believe that "If you think you can, you are right!" That is what your first step ought to be. You have got to start believing that you can dazzle like a diamond and this book is going to help you realise how you can!

And trust me, a belief can do wonders. You must believe you can. In fact, the worst thing in life is not that many people don't think they can, but that many people despite knowing that they can, still don't! For example, so many people know that they can protest when an injustice takes place. But cynicism holds them back. "What's the use?" they ask. "Nothing will change," they justify. I started my first book *Count Your Chickens Before They Hatch* with one quotation of Mahatma Gandhi, "Almost anything you do will seem insignificant. But it's very important that you do it. You must be the change you wish to see in this world." To

CARAT
Passion
Positive Energy

CUT
Performance
Perseverance

COLOUR
Personality
People Skills

CLARITY
Perspective
Principles
Patriotism

The Four Cs of Grading the

Human Diamond

me, discovering the diamond within us is not merely trying to do well for ourselves. It's about making a difference in society and making a better society. When we see so much wrong happening around us, we can get very critical – I often do get into that mode in my editorial columns in *The Sunday Indian*. But looking at the way our system functions, I also believe that the best way to feel good and change things around is by changing ourselves, and by being the change we want to see! Because there is hardly anything that we can't do if we want to. And that's the underlying philosophy of this process of 'discovering the diamond in you!'

Thus, if a diamond were to be the metaphor for human beings, then let's consider the four qualities which make a diamond so sought after. The first quality that makes a diamond so invaluable is its carat weight. You would have heard questions like, "How many carats is that diamond?" That's the most sought after quality of a diamond. In human beings, carats are the

9P
SUCCESS TRILLIANT

PASSION
POSITIVE ENERGY
PERFORMANCE
PERSEVERANCE
PERSONALITY
PEOPLE
PERSPECTIVE
PRINCIPLES
PATRIOTISM

Discover
the Diamond in
You

depth that we possess. And this is represented by two Ps: Passion and Positive Energy! These are the two most important aspects that are the hallmark of a diamond with a high carat value! All successful achievers have these two extremely important characteristics. The more the passion and positive energy inside you, the higher carat diamond you are!

The second quality that makes for a great diamond is its cut. The cut involves a lot of hard work. Thus, in human beings, the *cut* is about the next two Ps of this discovery process: Performance and Perseverance. If you want to have a great shine tomorrow and be sought after as a human diamond, then you have got to perform and have a tremendous amount of perseverance!

The third quality that makes a diamond visibly great is its colour. The more it refracts light, the higher it is priced. And exactly in the same way, a human being's colour is represented by the next two Ps: Personality and People Skills! The better these two are, the more light an individual refracts, the better is his colour, and the more he goes up in life.

And finally, the fourth quality that makes a diamond great is its clarity. In human beings, there are three Ps that represent clarity: Perspective, Principles and Patriotism. Without clarity, a diamond may seemingly dazzle, but under a lens, the dark spots become visible, and that takes away the value and sheen from the diamond. So, clarity — which manifests as the perspective about where and why the person is going, correct principles in life and a tremendous sense of patriotism — is what makes the human diamond really dazzle. The following pages will take you through each of these 9 Ps, which I call the '9P Success Trilliant' in order to enable you to understand their importance and help you succeed in life and dazzle!

HOW MANY CARATS IS THE DIAMOND WITHIN YOU?

There is nothing more powerful than a human soul on fire!

The first

P

of the
discovery:
PASSION

Nothing in life defines us more than how passionately we go about doing what we believe in. Like the density of a diamond is measured by its carats, similarly the depth of the human diamond lies in his passion. It is the most important ingredient for success and happiness in life! Without it, we are worth nothing; and as human diamonds, our carats would be negligible. Passion can make anything happen.

Follow your passion and everything will

follow. Take the case of the high school biology teacher who loved playing football and left everything to go on to become a football and sports coach in a university. Many would have considered it an ordinary, thankless job. Why do you think he chose to do it?

He realised that he was quite passionate about helping young athletes improve their performance while running.

He pursued this passion relentlessly and went on to become a coach of national and international stature.

But he did not rest on his laurels. His dedication and passionate will to succeed ensured his name in the *Hall of Fame* gallery as one of the greatest track and field coaches in the history of the United States, having trained some of the finest athletes who went on to become record holders and Olympic champions.

The fame and everything else that went with it was gratifying, but did not reduce his passion to keep improving the athletic performance.

He pushed himself to experiment and aggressively pursue inventive approaches.

His insatiable curiosity pushed him to realise that running shoes are an athlete's best friend and if only an ounce could be removed from the shoe's weight, then, in a one-mile race, almost 200 pounds of aggregate effort could be reduced.

His research found no takers among any of the shoe manufacturers, but that did not deter him at all.

He went on to invent a waffle sole which was far lighter and had a better grip than the ones that were manufactured at the time.

Yet again, no one paid heed to his invention, but he knew he had to help athletes perform better and that was all that mattered. With this in mind, he went on to become a shoe manufacturer himself with the little savings that he had.

Over time, along with Phil Knight, a middle-distance runner, he overcame many trials and tribulations and went on to establish one of the biggest and most successful brands in marketing history with the omnipresent swoosh logo. Yes, the same biology teacher became the co-founder of Nike, and like the brand, enjoyed a cult status of his own. And still his passion remained running and improving performance of athletes.

He wanted the world to share his passion. He ignited the jogging phenomenon in the United States. The term also became the title of his book, *Jogging*, selling a million plus copies. He helped define the sport of running as we know it today and helped people lead a better, healthy life derived from the joys and benefits of jogging.

One passion: Running.

And many facets: Educator, trainer, all-time great track and field legendary coach, ultra-innovator, inventor, brand builder, successful businessman, author and change agent.

That was Bill Bowerman for you. And trust me, your success story is waiting to happen, for there is a high carat diamond within you waiting to sparkle only if you are willing to ignite the passion within you and are ready to chase it passionately! And in this chase of your passion, there will be other powerful principles that will have to be followed. But nothing, absolutely nothing can be achieved without an unending strong passion! For chasing your passion is as good as discovering the diamond within you! You have to do what you believe in and you have to be passionate about what you are doing!

As Martin Luther King Jr said: If you are a street sweeper, so be it. Clean your street so well that others are forced to acknowledge your existence and feel that "here lived a street sweeper who did his job well," because anything worth doing is worth doing passionately. Else, neither will you be happy,

"He is so cold blooded that if a mosquito
bit him, it would die of pneumonia."

This ain't a diamond!

nor will you sparkle, and interestingly, nor will you earn money.

In the early 1960s, Srully Blotnik conducted a research on 1500 people. These people were divided into two groups and were observed for 20 years! Group A made up 83% of the sample and group B the remaining 17%. While the former lot embarked on a career chosen solely to make money, the latter chose a career based upon their passions and did what they wanted to do. In 1982, he published his research findings. At the end of twenty years, 101 people went on to become millionaires. Out of them, 100 were from the group which decided to follow their passions!

I surely don't need to say more about the importance of passion. All I can say is that all the other Ps that you will read about in the following chapters are either by-products of passion or play only a supportive role in success. Passion is all important and all pervasive.

Success occurs twice in life: Once in your mind and once in reality!

The second

P

of the
discovery:
POSITIVE ENERGY

Linked very closely to passion, the other characteristic which increases the carat of a human diamond is the positive energy that lies within us. The higher the positive energy, the more our chances of achieving success. All your passion can go waste, if it is not backed up by a tremendous amount of positive energy. That's the force behind our passions. And that's what makes passionate men work wonders!

What happens when a one-tonne boulder falls on you in a freak accident during a climbing expedition, and the doctor amputates both your legs from the mid-thigh? Well, if you have positive energy, then that is all that the doctor can take when you are Warren Macdonald, an adventure enthusiast with a more than rock solid passion for living and daring beyond the boundaries of acceptance. After a successful amputation operation that took away his legs but saved his life, the doctor announced to Warren that he would not be able to walk ever again. But the doctor never said anything about not cycling, kayaking or climbing, and totally underestimated the unbelievable power of positive energy that lay within this man! Thus, with tremendous positive energy to back up his undying passion for adventure, Warren went on to climb Africa's tallest peak Mt Kilimanjaro, America's tallest cliff face El Captain and Canada's Weeping Wall! That's the power of positive energy for you!

This positive energy has two sources. One is external motivation. Someone else motivates you and fills you with positive energy. Then, of course, the job is easier. But what when there is no source of external motivation? Well, that's when the real challenge comes. And that's when you look inside your own reserves and bring out your positivity. As Rabindra Nath Tagore wrote, "*Jodi tor dak shune keo na aashe, tobe ekla chalo re…* ['If nobody responds to your call, then walk it alone…']." That's the spirit of self-motivated men.

They motivate themselves and go after their dreams.

"By 1980, I will be the best known Oriental movie star in the United States and will have secured $10 million. And in return, I will give the very best acting I could possibly give every single time I am in front of the camera. And I will live in peace and harmony."

The above are contents of a secret letter that Bruce Lee wrote to himself. You can see it for

"When he finishes reading any mystery novel, he writes the name of the murderer on top of the first page before handing it to others."

This ain't a diamond!

yourself, if you ever visit Planet Hollywood in New York City.

The letter is dated 9 January 1970 and Bruce Lee died in 1973 after having surpassed all that he had decided for himself, much before the ten years' deadline he had set for himself. How many times have you written a letter to yourself? And made yourself a commitment and motivated yourself to go after it and excel? In my workshops all over the world, I always mention, "Success occurs twice in life. Once in your mind, in your beliefs and then once in reality." You can never be successful if you don't have the positive energy within you to believe that you can. It is a medical fact that when medicines fail, even cancer can be cured with the help of positive energy! And the best example of this is Lance Armstrong. Positive energy can even fight real physical problems to make you achieve the impossible, let alone any other problem.

Sustained Sincerity: The two most important words that make an achiever!

HOW WELL CUT IS THE DIAMOND WITHIN YOU?

Failure is not when you don't reach your goals. It is when you don't have any goal to reach!

The third

P

of the
discovery:
PERFORMANCE

"Continuing the same behaviour and expecting a different result," is how the organization Alcoholics Anonymous defines 'Insanity'. If you keep doing what you've always done, you'll keep getting what you've always got, and only a mad man would think otherwise. If you want things around you to change, you need to be that change agent. You have got do something more than what you've always been doing. You need to act – now! You need to perform and lead by example for others to follow. This is where the hard work begins. It's the true test of the cut of the diamond in you.

Doctors, psychologists, coaches, mentors and just about everybody maintained that it was humanly impossible to cross a mile in less than 4 minutes. Every athlete accepted this as a norm, but not Roger Bannister, who broke the barrier through sheer hard work. In 1954, hailed now as the miracle run, he defied all logic as he sped past 45 others runners and crossed the finishing line in 03:59:04 seconds. History was created that day because it was his hard work that gave shape to his passion. The high carat diamond had been cut very well! The very next year, about two dozen people crossed the mile in less than 4 minutes. Today, this is an expected norm.

George Washington Carver, a chemist who discovered over 325 uses for the peanut, once remarked, "99% of all failures come from people who have a habit of making excuses."

Simply said, there is no short cut to success. Nothing compares to the power of sincere and dedicated hard work. The best success stories have been scripted by individuals who have never shied away from hard work, and have performed when it mattered.

The route to success is a four stage plan – if you can vividly imagine, ardently desire, genuinely believe in your dreams and act upon them wholeheartedly, there is no one who can stop you. The funny part is, most of us are very good with imagining, passionately desiring and truly believing in our dreams, but most of us forget the 'act' bit. As someone rightly said, "Some people dream of success. Others wake up and work hard at it." That is the difficult part. You need to work, for the love of it.

Dreaming and believing is fine – it's the one who outperforms others, who wins. Anita Roddick, founder of The Body Shop, did not stop at just believing in the fact that one needed

"He is a well-known miracle worker!
It's a miracle when he works."

This ain't a diamond!

to work for the less privileged, she also went ahead and showed the world how. Visiting remote tribal communities around the world, searching for ingredients and then bringing them back to her research department to see if a beauty product could be created to make her Western consumers look and feel better, she developed a novel way of not just doing business but of helping the community too. She did whatever it required to connect with the tribals – travelling by elephants in India, distributing condoms to truckers entering red-light areas, even going to the extent of dropping her drawers to show some tribal women her pubic hair just to connect with them and clinch a deal.

"You can't cross the sea merely by standing and staring at the water," said Rabindranath Tagore. You need to be ready to go the extra mile. The secrets of success will not work until you do that.

Christopher Reeve charmed the world

with his performance in the *Superman* movie series, and in 1978, during the Academy Awards, wittily remarked that he had gained stardom only because he looked like a cartoon character. However, it was during the 1996 Academy Awards when the world actually saw the true 'Superman' Christopher Reeve, when he came to the award function in a wheelchair. A riding accident had left him paralyzed from the neck down. That day, not only did the Academy Award hall echo with thunderous applause from the audience, but the world over too, people marvelled at the man's indomitable spirit. Even a serious injury like that could not stop him from performing. He refused to let tragedy turn him into a martyr, and became a crusader for spinal cord injuries. He spoke to large crowds of 20,000 and motivated and inspired them. In fact, it's his 'real' life performance on stage that left a greater impact on the world than his 'reel' life ones. Truly a Superman!

You need to seize the day – make the most of every moment – for every moment matters. Bill Gates is the richest man in the world, and yet, even today, he works 16-18 hours every day. Malcolm Gladwell, in his new book *Outliers*, speaks of a study done in the 1990s by the psychologist K. Anders Ericsson, who studied musicians from Berlin's elite 'Academy of Music' and tracked the number of hours each top musician had practised during the past. Based on that, Gladwell reveals that it's nothing else but the number of hours of practice that differentiates world class performers from the not so good ones.

The magic number Gladwell reaches is 10,000 hours of practice. This is what is required to become a master at anything – music, painting, chess, sports . . . . Mozart produced his greatest compositions only after he had composed music for more than twenty years – by which time, he had put in the desired 10,000 hours. If you need to succeed, you need to start early in life – to be able to clock those 10,000 hours. Warren Buffet, the financial wizard, bought his first share at 11 years of age. Bill Gates wrote his first piece of software at the age of thirteen.

When he was 15, he scored 100 not out in his debut first class match for Bombay against Gujarat. He was the youngest Indian to score a century on first class debut. He has gone on to score over 30,000 runs in international cricket. Yes, the man is Sachin Tendulkar, whom Amitabh Bachchan called the 'nation's heartbeat,' which keeps beating till he is on the field and stops when he's out. It's the accolades that the world sees. What they forget is, when other children were enjoying the joys of childhood, Sachin as a little boy was practising day in and day out relentlessly at the nets.

Maniram Sharma, a son of an illiterate farmer from a remote village in Alwar didn't get deterred by his 100% hearing disability.

He became a merit holder in his tenth and twelfth boards, completed his Ph.D. and tried for 15 years before making it to the IAS! Thus, the fact remains that the only place where success comes before work is in a dictionary.

As the saying goes, talent is cheaper than table salt. It is most overrated. What separates the talented from the successful is the sheer dynamism of consistent hard work. A man who is energy, enigma personified, who electrifies the stage with his sheer presence – Shah Rukh Khan – is the best example of what persistent hard work and determination can do. Way back, heroes were tall, with booming voices. And without good connections, you couldn't survive in Bollywood. He defied all rules and sculpted his own success story – his way. He is a figure of admiration and is held in high esteem by all. Anyone who works with him knows that he has never failed to perform, and that's the proof of how well cut a diamond he really is.

The result of your journey is not the reward. The journey is the reward!

The fourth **P** of the discovery: **PERSEVERANCE**

"The only people who never fail are those who never try!" This quote sums up this 'P'. Show me a winner and I will show you how true the fallacy of the term 'overnight success' is. Every winner is a winner because he has dared to fail. Consider some of these stories:

- This man was turned down by Toyota Motor Corporation in a job interview for an engineer during World War II. Soichiro did not lose hope. He went on to start Honda.

- She was rejected by 20th Century Fox as they thought she was unattractive.

Little did Fox realize that even years after her death, Marilyn Monroe would remain the quintessential Hollywood diva everyone loves to love.

• His music teacher told him that as a composer, he was hopeless. Beethoven's music lives on even now!

They all showed the world one thing — if you believe in yourself, then irrespective of what the world says, you must have the perseverance to just keep doing what you think you can — and you will surely. The difference between successful persons and others is neither lack of strength, nor a lack of knowledge, but often, a lack of perseverance. In my organisation, Planman, every individual is extremely passionate. Yet, many often fail. And I've realised that almost every single time, the reason is lack of what I call "sustained sincerity," or in other words, perseverance. You can have a lot of passion and even deliver high value performance from time to time, but that actually is worth almost nothing in the long run. What matters is performing each and every time and with exactly as much sincerity. And then, you sure are a very well cut diamond; and mind you, it is the cut of a diamond which requires the hardest work!

Spielberg was put in a class for those with learning disabilities. Michael Jordan was taken out from his high school basketball team. Vincent Van Gogh sold only one painting in his lifetime. What made these ordinary failures into extraordinary success icons was their ability to persist – to persist when no one gave them a chance, to persevere when the world labelled them as failures.

J. K. Rowling is the world's first billionaire author; in fact, she faced such rejection that few of us would have experienced. An exceptionally short-lived marriage left her jobless – a single parent as poor as it was possible to be in modern Britain, she hit 'rock bottom'. It was this experience of hitting rock

"He sleeps 8 hours and works 8 hours. His boss is firing him because they are the same 8 hours."

This ain't a diamond!

bottom that became the solid foundation of her life. Failure taught her to stop pretending and doing what mattered most to her — writing. An old typewriter, a dear daughter and her imagination were all that she had to make do with to shine, and she did survive.

Richard Branson's Virgin Atlantic was a new airline with lots of promises, and a threat to its competitors. British Airways was a big, old player in this business, yet Virgin's entry made it feel the heat and it took recourse to every possible dirty trick to kill Virgin. It snooped into Virgin's confidential data and found out which of its flights were delayed, and then hired people who, with white carnations on their lapels, would go scouting for delayed Virgin passengers to persuade them to transfer to BA. For a tiny start-up like Virgin with a fleet of only seven aircraft, this was a big blow. Every passenger lost meant losses. As Branson admitted, "Had we only had the airline, we would have gone under . . . The strength of otherVirgin companies saved us." Yet, Branson did not give up. He fought back. He dared to file a case against this huge opponent for poaching its passengers. He won!

Kiran Majumdar Shaw started her company in her garage in Bangalore. She named it Biocon. It was in the business of making enzymes for industrial use. Back then, in the 1970s, no one understood enzymes and they definitely did not want to bet on a business if it had a woman as its head. Banks refused to loan her money without a male guarantor. She could not find anyone who was ready to work for her – not even a secretary. She did not cry foul and give up. She kept faith and stuck on till she found a bank that was willing to take a chance on her. In 2004, Biocon went public; and by the end of the first day of trading, the company had achieved a market value of $1.1 billion. Today, Kiran Majumdar Shaw is India's wealthiest woman.

Life can be quite a roller-coaster and Steve

Jobs, the co-founder of Apple Computers, knows it best. At the age of 21, he and his friend Steve Wozniak made their first computer in Jobs' garage in 1976. By the time Jobs was 25, he was worth $200 million and was featured on *TIME* magazine's cover at 26. In 1985, at the age of 30, he was thrown out of his own company by John Scully – the very man whom Jobs himself had recruited into Apple when Scully was the head of marketing at Pepsi.

Not many founders are made to resign from the very companies they have founded. Not to be dissuaded, Jobs immersed himself into the formation of a new company NEXT. It was a disaster. In the meanwhile, Apple realised it was a mistake to have let go of Steve Jobs and bought over NEXT, along with Jobs. The failure of NEXT did not worry Jobs for he then went on to form Pixar Inc. which created six of the biggest blockbuster animated films of all times, which together grossed more than $3.2 billion at box offices worldwide by

2005. These films made Jobs the most sought after man in Hollywood. The man went from success to success. His iPod (launched in 2003) and the digital jukebox iTunes changed the music industry of the world.

On 15 August 1992, Mani Ratnam's movie *Roja* was released. The movie was a hit, but there was something else that rocked the film. It was the music rendered by a shy quiet 25-year-old debutante, A. R. Rahman, who became a household name overnight – or so the world thought. What escaped notice was the years of hardships faced and gruelling hard work that this young lad had put in when his father unexpectedly passed away leaving the nine year old to take care of his mother and sisters.

Life sometimes proves to be a hard taskmaster and makes you put up with the worst. But as J. Paul Getty once said, "A man may fail many times, but he isn't a failure until he begins to blame somebody else." Stop complaining and take adversity in your stride.

Adversity of every kind is what Oprah Winfrey faced since the beginning. Born into a poor family, she was molested by male relatives and became pregnant at the tender age of 14. The girl carried on. Her job as a news anchor was not too successful either. She finally tasted her first success when she became the co-host on a local talk show. Her own talk show created history. It made her America's number one celebrity. Today, she is the most influential person in America. Not bad for a girl who received her first pair of shoes at age six. She's come a long way, done everything, save one – she didn't complain, or blame others or destiny.

Success teaches us very little – it is failure that makes you think and work harder.

Be prepared to fail, but have the perseverance to try again and again. Success will not be far behind.

There has never been a great leader without a great personality.

WHAT IS THE COLOUR OF THE DIAMOND WITHIN YOU?

"He has never been known to say an unkind word about anyone – that's because he only talks about himself."

This ain't a diamond!

The fifth

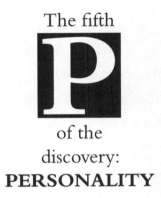

of the
discovery:
PERSONALITY

The colour of the human diamond is determined by an individual's personality and faith in one of the most important Ps for success – Personality. A charismatic and pleasing personality is one major aspect of success. Personality hones in you the synergy effect. Add a magnetic personality to your hard work and perseverance and you can reach much further than you can with hard work alone.

It's not just great talent but a feeling of camaraderie and commitment within a team that leads to its success. This can only happen when there is a leader who not only leads from the front, but also loves his team; who understands each team member the most and gives each one a task where the individual can excel.

In a leader, personality is more important than technical expertise. He has to have this ability to create an aura of dynamism around him and bring in so much good cheer and positive energy that it sets the right tone for the entire organisation and has a strong, positive impact on group performance.

To become such a great leader and develop a magnetic personality, you need to work day in and day out and groom yourself. You need to become a great communicator and relentlessly follow the LAW of personality building.

And the law of personality stands for Looks, Actions and Words! These are the three hallmarks of a great personality. 'Looks' is not about how good looking you are physically – because there is nothing like good looking and bad looking (What's 'good looking' in America may be bad looking in Africa; what's good looking in Africa might be bad looking in Vietnam; and what's good looking in Vietnam may be considered ugly in India!). 'Looks' is about the first impression you give of yourself to others, from the way you present yourself.

A United Nations summit is the best example of how leaders of a hundred plus nations – all with different physical looks – come across as looking so good. Why? Because regardless of the colour of your skin and your physical appearance, when you stand in the UN summit wearing a white shirt, a fitting black suit, a red tie, well-polished shoes and hair neatly done, you are bound to make a good impression. It doesn't cost much either, but it decides if the other person is interested in speaking to you. Often, during an interview, from the time you walk into the room and take your seat, the interviewer has already decided not to take you. That's because he is searching for a surrogate for his organisation; and just by looking at you, he might have decided he doesn't need you. And you are left wondering why you were asked only two questions before the interviewer let you go? So, the first impression that you make is very important in life.

After looks, come your actions: The way you walk, the way you use your hands while speaking, the way you take the chair to sit, the way you use eye contact while speaking... Everything is important! Because what you have inside you is first reflected by your looks and then by your actions. It's only when you have been able to make a favourable impression with your looks and actions that you are given a chance to use the 'W' of LAW, that is, your words. So, we must remember that despite having great knowledge, we might never even be heard, if we aren't able to use our looks and actions properly before uttering any words!

Years after the first time that Dr Prannoy Roy broke into our drawing rooms, he is still one man whom we love to watch. Ever wondered why? That's because there are very few people on television who can match better his polished looks, amazing body language, actions and articulate and intelligent words. It's the same reason why we love to see Rajdeep Sardesai or Arnab Goswami – again Dr Roy's proteges – on TV.

When STAR TV's fortunes were dwindling, they roped in Amitabh Bachchan. He stormed into our drawing rooms with his immaculate personality – a perfect example of the power of LAW of personality – and bowled us over. Talent apart, it's his personality that took him to a level that no one else had ever reached before, despite there being many other very talented people before him, including some superstars too!

The job of the leader is not to create followers. It is to create more leaders. Fearlessly.

The sixth

P

of the
discovery:
PEOPLE

During interviews, I am often asked how I manage an institute, a media house, a film production company and a consulting firm, all together. I always say — and I mean it — "I have got great people who run my businesses, and I just give interviews!"

The truth is that if I were to do it alone, I wouldn't have been able to do a fraction of what we do. But because I have a team of extremely passionate people, a considerable lot gets done. That's the power of believing in people. I have always believed that the most important job of a leader is to find his replacement. Only then can he grow in life. The graveyards, as they say, are full of people who thought they were indispensable and could do it all by themselves.

It's a big, bad, mad world out there, and in this rat race for success, you are competing with people who are equally, if not more talented than you, and as competitive and determined. The way to take the lead then is to have with you a great team. There is an African saying, "If you want to go fast, go alone; if you want to go far, go together." You need to have the ability and the knack of building a great team. It's easy to get good players, but getting them to play together is the hard part.

He was a railroad conductor's son, who as a child, suffered from a stuttering problem. Not many would have called him a leader, yet it's this man's might that made GE one of the top ranking companies in the world. When asked about the secret of his success, Jack Welsh said, "Great people, not great strategies, are what made it all work!" 'Teamwork' works, and it's no secret. Years ago, Thomas Edison was asked why he had a team of twenty-one assistants. He replied, "If I could solve all the problems myself, I would."

Nature is at its ferocious best on the Himalayas — ask any mountain climber and he will have his share of horror stories to tell. Small and helpless, in front of the powers of nature, mountaineers rely on one indispensable ally — other mountaineers. For any successful climbing mission, teamwork is essential. It was the strong bond of friendship and trust that was, among other factors, responsible for the success of the first ascent of Everest. Sir Edmund Hillary and Tenzing Norgay would probably have not been able to do it alone in spite of being highly talented individually. Much similar to Michael Jordan, who in spite of being supremely talented, failed to win

"He is such a pain in everyone's neck that the Aspirin people are thinking of giving him royalty."

This ain't a diamond!

the NBA championship till he got a team that complemented him. If there is one sport where success depends on the power to work in a team, it's basketball. Five players working together is a perfect setting for getting that ultimate teamwork-experience. Be it business or sports, the rules of success remain more or less the same. Look at Infosys and you have a classic example of the powers of teamwork. It was a great team (including Nandan Nilekani and Kris Gopalakrishnan along with Narayana Murthy) that, with its hard work and commitment, could build one of India's greatest companies from scratch. Many people knew that India had a vast pool of English speaking, analytically strong, technically talented personnel with great work ethics (the perfect ingredients for global success). Yet, it was only one man and his team who were able to harness this energy, this pool of talent and nurture it into a big business house. Murthy understood the benefits of teamwork very early.

When his father taught him Western classical music, he also showed Murthy how in Western classical music, a group of people – maestros in their own right – came together, overcame their egos, and worked as a team to produce something outstanding. Something that each one individually would never have been able to do. Who could understand teamwork better than Vince Lombardi, the one time football coach for NFL. He said, "Teamwork is what the Green Bay Packers were all about. They didn't do it for individual glory. They did it because they loved one another . . ."

It can easily be said that there are plenty of success stories with only the first four Ps. But when you add Personality and People Skills, it has a synergy effect and 1+1 is no more 2; it becomes 11! If you want to multiply your success score, you have to focus on the colour of the human diamond!

WHAT IS THE CLARITY OF THE DIAMOND WITHIN YOU?

"Scientists say fog can now be made to order . . .
This is hardly news to him."

This ain't a diamond!

The seventh

of the
discovery:
PERSPECTIVE

Perspective is the first P that helps us become a spotless clear diamond! If you know where you are travelling to and what you want in life, everything else becomes clear, and your journey reaps the maximum rewards. Perspective requires personal as well as a broader vision. The unfortunate reality in our lives is that often, because we lack perspective, we choose that path which gives us short-term returns, but is harmful in the long run. Every year, during the government budget exercise, the entire Indian business community, without fail, displays its complete lack of perspective for themselves as well as for the country. They go to the finance minister and lobby for short-term gains through reduction of petty taxes here and there. Removal of poverty and providing purchasing power to the poor is never in the agenda they wish to lobby for. Such a misdirected perspective not only harms the nation immensely, but most importantly harms their own business too. Due to a total lack of perspective, our business community doesn't realise the same. Nokia, Electrolux, HP, and similar other corporations sell far more in China than in India. Why? Because the Chinese people have purchasing power and the government works sincerely to lift them out of poverty. Today, we virtually live in a world owned by the Chinese. Indian leaders – especially in business – due to their lack of perspective, fail to realise that if the government were to focus on poverty eradication, their own products would sell tens of times more, and their profits would increase far more than what they would gain by lobbying for a percentage reduction in excise duty. That's what I mean by perspective. We all need it in life to know our way forward.

Ray Kroc was a salesman who, for a decade and a half, sold multi-mixers to make milkshakes. His largest customer was a California-based restaurant that used a mass production-cum-assembly line for making hamburgers and sandwiches. He convinced the brothers who owned the company to sell the restaurant to him. At the age of 52, while suffering from diabetes and arthritis, with his gallbladder and thyroid gland having been surgically removed, Ray Kroc was never more sure in his life about what he wanted to do. The McDonald brothers were so busy working that they missed out on the long-term potential of their plan. It required Ray Kroc's vision to make McDonald's the way we know it today.

A clear perspective gives you the insight and the guts to believe in your dreams and carry on. It was Mahatma Gandhi's vision that helped free India. He knew it was only and only through his 'Satyagraha' non-violent movement that India could appeal to the moral conscience of Britain and make the British realize the unfairness of colonial Raj.

It was Ted Turner's vision and his ability to see the big picture that made him think out of the box to give birth to CNN. Cable news changed the way the world watched news.

Sitting in his dorm room in Harvard, Mark Zuckerberg saw the immense potential of an online 'social graph'. Instead of using the Internet to make new friends the way Myspace does, he thought it would be more fun just keeping in touch with old friends and acquaintances. It was this plan that helped him launch Facebook, which has today become a giant new powerful model of word of mouth communication. It was like meeting friends and family and conversing with them around a dinner table – only this time, you did it online with a mouse, not your mouth.

People thought Jeff Bezos was crazy – after all, who would buy books online. His amazon. com proved them wrong. His latest invention, Kindle (the e-reader) was mocked at too. Who wanted to read from a screen? Well, too many I guess, considering the fact that Amazon ran out of Kindles in just a few hours after its launch in November 2008.

Meg Whitman saw the strong potential for technology that could "change lives" and provide a level playing field where a new entrepreneur could compete with a large corporation in selling goods. E-bay grew from 30 employees to 15,000 with $8 billion in revenue under the visionary leadership of Meg Whitman.

One wintry day in 1990, the founders of Infosys met in a small office. The excitement this time was something new. After nine years of toiling hard, the company had received an enticing offer — a sum of $1 million for selling Infosys. For hours, everyone discussed animatedly how this would prove to be a turning point in their careers, and how with the extra money, they could all move on. Finally, when it was Murthy's turn to speak, he reminded them of the dream with which they had started the company and said that even if times were hard at the time, things would change if they had faith. The darkest hours came just before dawn. It was Murthy's long-term perspective and foresight that made Infosys what it is today.

Sergey Brin was a senior in Stanford University where he met Larry Page. Even though their first meeting started with arguments, it was their common vision about the potential of the web that led them to lay the foundation of Google — the largest search engine of the world.

The right perspective often makes the real

difference in the long run. "A PC on every desk in every home," propelled Microsoft in the right direction for many years.

On a much lighter note, after being inspired by a bout between Muhammad Ali and Chuck Wepner, Sylvester Stallone wrote the screenplay for *Rocky*. Many producers liked the script and were ready to pay him a lot of money for it but refused his condition to cast him as well. Even with the lure of USD 265,000 at a time when his bank balance was only USD 100, Stallone refused to lose his perspective till he got what he wanted. *Rocky* was a runaway success and Stallone was nominated for ten Academy Awards.

A clear perspective gives you the power and courage to face even the greatest of problems with optimism. It becomes the source of greatest motivation during your darkest hours. A clear perspective shows you the direction to follow when life brings you to a crossroad.

Let there never be any doubt about what you stand for.

The eighth

P

of the
discovery:
PRINCIPLES

The second P in our lives that helps us become spotless clear diamonds is our principles. As a consultant to some leading organisations, I have realised that the biggest challenge at the top level that leaders face in finding a second man for themselves is the lack of principles and ethics in people. For, by the time they reach the top, they realise that those are principles that make a man stand tall in the long run, contrary to the popular belief that one needs to be street smart in life – another way of saying one needs to sacrifice principles in life — to move ahead fast. It's actually not true. All great leaders worth naming, worth appreciating, have always stuck to their principles. That's what takes them to the very top. Sacrifice principles and you've put a big spot inside the diamond that will be revealed one day or the other. That's why it's most important for us to know the real definition of success. Success is not about the results. Success is about the courage to undertake a journey that you believe in, as the title of Steve Jobs' book says, "*The journey is the reward.*" That's the true meaning of success for a principled man. And that's what the *Gita* explains beautifully, "*Tu karm kiye ja, phal ki chinta mat kar* [Keep working without worrying about the results]." Yes, that's what true diamonds do. They keep doing what they believe in, what they know is right, without worrying about results. Some like Subhash Chandra Bose or Che Guevara never saw success. But that doesn't mean that they were failures. They tried and chased what they believed in. And for them, the journey was the reward. We must believe this and then we can never experience failure. For the man to whom the journey itself is the reward, everything else is merely an add-on. And that's how we become clear diamonds.

For decades, this man was denied the simple pleasure of watching the sun set — a view that used to fill him with the greatest happiness. Nelson Mandela is a man who personifies struggles. He spent nearly three decades of his life behind bars, endured hardships, yet never ever did he compromise on his principles. It was this that inspired others around him and gave them strength and optimism.

Individuals and corporations need to live by a set of values. A brand becomes famous and loved only when the leader behind it shows integrity. Starbucks is so big because Howard Schultz ensured every cup of coffee made in his outlet was of the best quality, because

"He is so crooked, when he dies they will
have to screw him to the ground."

This ain't a diamond!

cutting corners could lead only to short-term success.

Her party won 82% of the seats in the 1990 elections, but the Junta regime refused to hand over power. Instead, it imprisoned and tortured members of her party and put Aung San Suu Kyi under house arrest. The Junta could arrest her but not stop her, and today her struggle remains one of the most extraordinary examples of civil courage.

It's a wrong notion that to succeed you need to be unethical. J.R.D Tata, India's most respected businessman for decades, showed the world how one could succeed in business while maintaining very high ethical standards. Never did he bribe politicians or use the black market to increase revenues. Today, the TATA group remains India's most respected business house. Contrast this to the Satyam, Enron or recently the Bernard Madoff scam – all their top men are behind bars. This only shows that in the long run, it pays to be ethical.

Inglorious is that success, which comes without patriotism.

The ninth

of the
discovery:
PATRIOTISM

The final P of this discovery of the diamond in you is patriotism! It is the final symbol of clarity of the human diamond. The most dazzling of clear human diamonds, without patriotism, will always show up dark spots, when viewed under a magnifying lens! You might be a high carat diamond which has been cut meticulously and has a great colour, but it's the love for your country and for human beings anywhere in the world that makes a human diamond perfect! Patriotism makes your success live forever. In the mid-1950s,

Akio Morita, the man behind Sony, rejected a huge order of a hundred thousand units for his transistor radios at a time when he was struggling to find any takers for his products, because the buyers said he could not brand his radio. For Akio, his country came first. Five years later, while walking on New York's Fifth Avenue, Akio realised that many nations except Japan had their flags on display on top of the avenue's stores. He made it his mission to fly the first Japanese flag there. Two years later, 1962 became a hallmark year as it was the first time since World War II that the Japanese flag was unfurled formally on American soil. What a day it must have been! Sony was able to make the world look up to Japan. And the rest, as they say, is history.

It was this patriotic fervour that made Nobel laureate Muhammad Yunus start the Grameen Bank in Bangladesh. He gave loans to poor women, who were the most neglected group in his country!

His poor borrowers today are better at repaying their loans than many of the rich who borrow from big banks!

It's the same feeling with which Samuel Casas started Casas Bahia, an organisation in Brazil that runs with the sole aim of increasing the standard of living of Brazilians – especially of those below the poverty line. It's an organisation with its heart at the right place. Explaining his stance, Samuel says, "My talent is trusting the poor and giving them good service. Many poor have a better character than the rich. I was poor once."

The Chinese today have turned their backs on all things Western – from designer wear to cars. The no. 1 selling car in China is Chery, the no. 1 selling cola in rural China is the Chinese company Wa Ha Ha's Future Cola. Be it these two or China Mobile, Gree Electronics, Haier or Lenovo – behind all these success stories is a story of patriotism and the urge to make the Chinese flag fly high! On the contrary, while

"His commitment to his country is legendary. When he is dead many people will attend his funeral to make absolutely sure that he is dead."

This ain't a diamond!

India has amongst the maximum billionaires in the *Forbes* top hundred billionaires list, unfortunately India doesn't have a single brand in the top hundred list of global brands. There is no other P that is worth sacrificing more for in life, business, sports or politics than patriotism.

It is this urge to bring glory to India that made Dronacharya Award winner, Jagdish Singh, boxing coach of Olympic medalist Vijendra Singh, start the Bhiwani boxing club with his provident fund money and a 4 lac rupee loan from the Gramin Bank. Single-handedly, he brought glory to India. Three of his students qualified for the quarter finals at the 2008 Beijing Olympics.

The world's greatest ever revolutionary, Che Guevara, was an Argentinian who fought for the Cuban revolution, left his ministerial post in Cuba to go and fight for Congo, and Bolivia – where he finally met his end. For him, the world where there was any exploitation was his home. He lost most of the wars he fought. But he was a sparkling diamond like no other. The great Frenchman Satre called him not only an intellectual, but also the most complete human being of our age. Che said, "Failure does not necessarily mean that the cause you were fighting for was not worth it." A graffiti scrawl in Spanish on the wall of the public telephone office in the little town of Vallegrande in Bolivia where Che was executed, reads: "Che – alive, as they never wanted you to be!"

If you want to find that dazzling and clear diamond within you, never forget to love your country and the people of the world on the whole, especially the underprivileged and the exploited. Life becomes worth living when patriotism is what drives your passions. And the discovery of the diamond within you becomes complete!

YOU ARE A DIAMOND! NOW DAZZLE!

In trying times, never stop trying! After all, the word 'diamond' originates from the Greek word 'adamas', meaning unconquerable!

YOU ARE A DIAMOND! NOW DAZZLE!

In trying times, never stop trying! After all, the word 'diamond' originates from the Greek word 'adamas', meaning unconquerable!

I hope you now know the powerful principles of discovering the diamond in you. You are a diamond! And now, all you have to do is never miss out on any of these 9 points in exactly the same sequence. Of course, that's not to say that the last few Ps are not as important as the initial ones – in fact, I mentioned in the previous chapter that patriotism is worth sacrificing the most for! But having said that, it is true that even without patriotism, you can be successful; it's just that your success won't be as glorious. And lastly, never forget that more than the final outcome – as I wrote in the chapter on principles – success is about the passionate effort that you put in trying to do what you believe in. The results will always follow, especially when you have put into practice all these 9Ps. Now go ahead. Practice them. And dazzle in life!

TO READ ARINDAM CHAUDHURI'S
WEEKLY THOUGHTS
LOG ON TO
arindamchaudhuri.blogspot.com

TO INTERACT WITH ARINDAM CHAUDHURI
LOG ON TO
www.facebook.com/pages/Arindam-Chaudhuri/76429890015

TO ORGANISE ARINDAM CHAUDHURI'S
INSPIRING SESSIONS WITH YOUR ORGANISATION

CALL NOW AT +91 9811270918
e-mail : chanda.mehra@planmanconsulting.com

THE INDIAN INSTITUTE OF
PLANNING & MANAGEMENT

THE ROOTS

The year 1963, a dream – a proposal to Pt. Jawaharlal Nehru, the then Prime Minister of India, to set up an institute under the name of 'Institute for Planning and Administration of National Economy'; A study tour of Europe and a man – the roots of an institute with a difference; an institute oriented towards the promotion of corporate growth, based on innovation and entrepreneurship in harmony with national economic planning objectives, aiming at a sustainable and ethically acceptable growth rate. This was conceptualised by an eminent professor of IIM Bangalore, Dr MK Chaudhuri. He travelled extensively across Europe to study similar institutions and The Indian Institute of Planning and Management was formally registered in the year 1973.

TO KNOW MORE ABOUT IIPM AND

What progress has there been since the year 1973 . . .

What makes IIPM the most unique institute in the country . . .

What makes the maximum number of students join IIPM every year and remain crazy about it . . .

Which paper Prof. Arindam Chaudhuri is teaching in the current semester . . .

log on to www.iipm.edu